CODING WITH AI FOR BEGINNERS

How to Use Artificial Intelligence to Learn Coding, Build Projects, and Solve Problems

RODGERS DIAZ

Copyright © 2024 by Rodgers Diaz

All rights reserved. No part of this book may be reproduced or transmitted in any form or by any means, electronic or mechanical, including photocopying, recording, or by any information storage and retrieval system, without permission in writing from the publisher.

The information provided in this book is designed to provide helpful information on the subjects discussed. The author and publisher disclaim any liability or loss in connection with the use or misuse of this information. It is recommended that readers consult with appropriate professionals before taking any actions based on the information in this book.

TABLE OF CONTENTS

CHAPTER 1 13

   THE IMPORTANCE OF AI IN MODERN CODING 13

      AI's Transformation of Software Development and Coding 14

      AI-Driven Tools and Technologies 15

      Benefits of Integrating AI into Modern Coding Practices 17

CHAPTER 2 21

   INTRODUCTION TO PROGRAMMING LANGUAGES FOR AI 21

      Overview of Popular AI Programming Languages .. 22

      Setting Up Your Coding Environment 30

      Introduction to Basic Coding Concepts 35

      Writing Your First Program 39

      Variables and Data Types in Action 41

      Using AI to Help with Coding 43

CHAPTER 3 47

   PYTHON BASICS WITH AI ASSISTANCE 47

      Basic Data Structures in Python 48

Chat Gpt Prompt Sample 57

Practical Problems for Practice 60

CHAPTER 4 63

DEBUGGING CODE WITH CHATGPT 63

What is Debugging? 64

Common Coding Errors and How to Resolve Them 66

Common Pitfalls in Python 70

Using ChatGPT to Debug Code 78

Debugging Tools and Techniques 83

CHAPTER 5 95

ADVANCED CODING TECHNIQUES WITH CHATGPT 95

Working with Databases and APIs 96

Writing Algorithms and Data Structures 109

Web Development with ChatGPT 116

Best Practices and Pitfalls to Avoid When Coding with ChatGPT 129

Conclusion 132

INTRODUCTION

In today's fast-paced, technology-driven world, the importance of learning to code cannot be overstated. Coding, the language of the future, opens doors to a myriad of job opportunities, bring up essential problem-solving skills, and facilitates the integration of technology across diverse fields. Whether you're looking to start a career in tech, enhance your current role, or simply keep up with the ever-evolving digital world, coding is a priceless skill.

The job market reflects this growing demand for coding proficiency. Industries ranging from healthcare to finance, entertainment to education, are increasingly reliant on software and digital solutions. Companies are on the lookout for individuals who can develop, maintain, and improve these technological systems. Proficient coders often find themselves in well-paid, secure positions with room for growth and innovation. Moreover, coding skills extend beyond traditional tech roles. They are now fundamental in data analysis, digital marketing, project management, and even creative industries like game design and multimedia arts.

Beyond job prospects, coding supports critical problem-solving abilities. It teaches you how to break down complex problems into manageable steps, think logically, and devise efficient solutions. These skills are universally applicable, making you a better thinker and problem-solver in any domain. Furthermore, as technology floods every aspect of our lives, a basic understanding of coding can empower you to better sail across and contribute to the digital world, whether it's automating mundane tasks or creating a personal website.

Amidst this backdrop of technological integration and the need for coding literacy, artificial intelligence (AI) has emerged as a transformative force in education. AI is revolutionizing traditional learning models, offering new ways to engage with and master complex subjects like coding. The rise of AI in education is not just a trend but a significant shift towards more personalized, efficient, and accessible learning.

Several key developments and milestones have marked AI's presence in education. Initially, AI tools were used to automate administrative tasks, such as grading and scheduling, thus freeing up educators to focus more on teaching. However, as AI technologies advanced, their applications in education expanded. Intelligent tutoring systems, adaptive learning platforms, and AI-driven educational games have since become integral components of modern learning environments. These tools can analyze students' learning patterns, predict their needs, and provide tailored resources to enhance their understanding and retention of material.

One of the most significant benefits of using AI tools for learning coding is the personalization they offer. Traditional classrooms often struggle to cater to the individual learning paces and styles of each student. AI addresses this challenge by providing customized learning experiences. For instance, AI-driven platforms can assess your current coding skills, identify gaps in your knowledge, and curate personalized learning paths that align with your pace and preferences. This means you can focus on areas where you need improvement, without wasting time on concepts you already understand.

Another major advantage of AI in coding education is real-time feedback. When learning to code, immediate feedback on your code's functionality and efficiency is crucial. AI tools can instantly analyze your code, highlight errors, suggest improvements, and even explain the underlying concepts. This immediate feedback loop accelerates the learning process, helping you quickly grasp new concepts and avoid common pitfalls. For example, platforms like CodeSignal and LeetCode use AI to provide detailed feedback on coding challenges, allowing users to learn from their mistakes and refine their skills effectively.

AI also makes coding more accessible for beginners. Traditional coding education can be daunting, often requiring a steep learning curve and a significant time investment. AI tools simplify this process by offering interactive, user-friendly interfaces and guided tutorials. For instance, platforms like Scratch and Blockly use AI to help beginners understand coding fundamentals through visual programming environments. These platforms allow users to create programs by manipulating graphical blocks, making it easier to grasp basic concepts before transitioning to text-based coding.

Overview of AI Tools: ChatGPT, Google Bard, and More

As artificial intelligence is rapidly evolving, tools like ChatGPT and Google Bard have become powerful resources for a wide range of users. Developed by leading tech giants OpenAI and Google respectively, these AI-driven tools offer versatile functionalities that assist users in tasks such as coding, content creation, problem-solving, research, and creative writing.

ChatGPT, developed by OpenAI, is an advanced language model built on the GPT-4 architecture. It's designed to understand and generate human-like text based on the input it receives. This capability makes ChatGPT incredibly versatile, useful in many contexts. For instance, it can assist with coding by helping users write, debug, and optimize code. Imagine you're working on a Python project and run into an error; you can describe the issue to ChatGPT, and it will suggest solutions or alternative approaches to fix the problem. Additionally, ChatGPT excels in content creation. Whether you need to draft a blog post, compose an email, or generate creative content, you can provide a topic or an outline, and ChatGPT will deliver well-structured and coherent text tailored to your needs. Beyond these applications, ChatGPT is also a powerful tool for problem-solving. It can help you think through complex problems by offering insights, proposing different approaches, and even helping with brainstorming sessions by generating new ideas and solutions. For example, a developer might use ChatGPT to write a snippet of code, a marketer could draft a compelling product description, and an entrepreneur might explore business concepts with its help.

On the other hand, Google Bard (Now called Gemini), developed by Google, is another sophisticated AI language model designed to assist users in various tasks. Leveraging Google's vast information network and advanced AI algorithms, Google Bard provides accurate and detailed responses. One of its key strengths is in aiding research. For example, a student working on a thesis can ask Google Bard to summarize recent studies on a particular topic, providing a comprehensive overview that saves time and effort. It also excels in content summarization. If a business analyst needs a quick summary of a lengthy market report, Google Bard can condense the information into concise summaries, making it easier to digest and understand. Moreover, Google Bard is a valuable tool for creative writing. An author experiencing writer's block can input the main idea of a story, and Google Bard will suggest plot developments, character arcs, and dialogues, helping to spark creativity and move the writing process forward.

While both ChatGPT and Google Bard are designed to assist users in various tasks, they have unique strengths and approaches. ChatGPT is particularly strong in interactive problem-solving and generating extensive, coherent content based on prompts. Its use cases often include coding assistance and detailed content creation, making it ideal for those who need to produce substantial amounts of text or engage in iterative feedback processes. Google Bard, by contrast, excels in summarizing large volumes of information and providing concise overviews. This makes it an excellent tool for research and quick content summarization, especially when you need reliable and up-to-date information quickly.

In terms of user interaction, ChatGPT is highly interactive and can engage in detailed back-and-forth conversations. This capability is beneficial for tasks that require iterative feedback and refinement, such as debugging code or brainstorming ideas. Google Bard also offers interactive capabilities but focuses more on providing clear, concise responses and summaries. This approach is particularly useful for quick reference and research purposes, where you need to digest information rapidly.

Unique aspects of each tool further highlight their strengths. ChatGPT's ability to generate human-like, creative, and extensive text outputs makes it ideal for diverse content creation needs, from technical writing to creative storytelling. On the other hand, Google Bard's integration with Google's search capabilities allows it to provide highly accurate and up-to-date information summaries, drawing from a vast array of sources across the web.

CHAPTER 1

THE IMPORTANCE OF AI IN MODERN CODING

AI'S TRANSFORMATION OF SOFTWARE DEVELOPMENT AND CODING

Artificial Intelligence (AI) is not only transforming industries like healthcare, finance, and transportation; it's also revolutionizing the field of software development and coding. AI is enhancing the traditional approach to coding, which often involves manual coding, debugging, and optimization, in ways that improve efficiency, accuracy, and innovation.

AI is reshaping software development in several profound ways. First, it automates routine and repetitive tasks, freeing up developers to focus on more complex and creative aspects of coding. Second, AI enhances the accuracy of code by detecting and fixing errors more efficiently than humans. Third, it helps in optimizing code for better performance, ensuring that applications run smoothly and effectively.

Imagine a world where writing code feels more like collaborating with a highly skilled assistant who can predict your needs, suggest improvements, and handle mundane tasks. AI is bringing this reality to the field of software development. AI-driven tools and technologies are becoming indispensable, enabling developers to create robust, high-quality software more quickly and with fewer errors.

AI-DRIVEN TOOLS AND TECHNOLOGIES

Various AI-driven tools and technologies facilitate the integration of AI into coding practices. These tools leverage machine learning algorithms, natural language processing, and other AI techniques to assist developers in multiple stages of the software development lifecycle.

Intelligent Code Editors

Intelligent code editors, such as Visual Studio Code with its AI-powered IntelliCode, provide smart suggestions to developers as they type. These editors analyze the context of the code and offer relevant code completions, making the coding process faster and reducing the likelihood of syntax errors. For instance, IntelliCode can suggest the most likely method or variable name based on the code context, significantly speeding up the coding process.

Automated Code Review Tools

AI-powered code review tools like DeepCode and Codacy use machine learning algorithms to analyze code for potential issues, including bugs, security vulnerabilities, and code quality problems. These tools provide developers with actionable feedback and suggestions for improvement, ensuring that code adheres to best practices and standards. Automating the code review process reduces the time and effort required for manual code reviews.

Bug Detection and Fixing Tools

AI-driven bug detection tools, such as Sentry and Bugsnag, help developers identify and fix bugs more efficiently. These tools use machine learning to analyze error patterns and predict where bugs are likely to occur. They also provide insights into the root causes of bugs, allowing developers to address issues more effectively. For example, Sentry can pinpoint the exact line of code causing an error and suggest potential fixes.

Automated Testing Tools

Automated testing is another area where AI is making a significant impact. Tools like Testim and Applitools leverage AI to create, execute, and maintain test cases. These tools can automatically generate test scripts based on user interactions, detect visual and functional anomalies, and adapt to changes in the application. This reduces the time and effort required for manual testing and ensures that applications are thoroughly tested before deployment.

AI-Powered Code Generation

AI-powered code generation tools, such as OpenAI's Codex and GitHub Copilot, are pushing the boundaries of what is possible in coding. These tools can generate entire blocks of code based on natural language descriptions or partial code snippets. For instance, you can describe a function in plain English, and GitHub Copilot will generate the corresponding code. This capability accelerates the coding process and makes it accessible to those with less programming experience.

BENEFITS OF INTEGRATING AI INTO MODERN CODING PRACTICES

The integration of AI into modern coding practices offers numerous benefits, enhancing the overall efficiency, accuracy, and creativity of software development.

1. **Automation of Routine Tasks**

One of the most significant benefits of AI in coding is the automation of routine tasks. Developers spend a considerable amount of time on repetitive tasks such as code formatting, refactoring, and testing. AI can automate these tasks, allowing developers to focus on more complex and value-added activities. This not only speeds up the development process but also improves job satisfaction by reducing the monotony of routine work.

2. Error Reduction and Improved Code Quality

AI-driven tools excel at detecting and fixing errors, which leads to improved code quality. Automated code review and bug detection tools can identify potential issues early in the development process, preventing them from becoming costly and time-consuming problems later on. This proactive approach to error detection ensures that code is more robust, secure, and maintainable.

3. Enhanced Problem-Solving Capabilities

AI enhances problem-solving capabilities by providing developers with insights and recommendations that they might not have considered. For example, AI-powered tools can suggest alternative algorithms or optimization techniques based on the context of the code. This helps developers solve complex problems more efficiently and explore innovative solutions.

4. **Accelerated Development Cycles**

The automation and efficiency gains provided by AI lead to accelerated development cycles. By reducing the time required for coding, testing, and debugging, AI allows teams to deliver software faster without compromising on quality. This is particularly beneficial in agile development environments, where quick iterations and rapid delivery are essential.

5. **Increased Accessibility and Inclusivity**

AI-powered code generation tools lower the barrier to entry for coding, making it more accessible to individuals with limited programming experience. By enabling users to generate code from natural language descriptions, these tools democratize coding and empower a broader range of people to create software. This inclusivity promotes a diverse community of developers, bringing new perspectives and ideas to the field.

CHAPTER 2

INTRODUCTION TO PROGRAMMING LANGUAGES FOR AI

OVERVIEW OF POPULAR AI PROGRAMMING LANGUAGES

PYTHON

Strengths:

Python is often the go-to language for AI development, and for good reason. It's known for its simplicity and readability, making it an excellent choice for beginners. The language has a vast ecosystem of libraries and frameworks specifically designed for AI and machine learning, such as TensorFlow, Keras, PyTorch, and scikit-learn. These tools make it easier to implement complex algorithms and build sophisticated AI models.

One of Python's greatest strengths is its community support. The AI and machine learning community around Python is vast and active, providing a wealth of resources, tutorials, and forums where you can seek help and share knowledge. This can be incredibly beneficial when you're learning the ropes of AI development.

Weaknesses:

While Python is versatile and user-friendly, it does have some limitations. Its interpreted nature can make it slower compared to compiled languages like C++ or Java, which might be a concern for time-sensitive applications.

Additionally, Python's dynamic typing can sometimes lead to runtime errors that are harder to debug.

Use Cases and Applications:

Python is widely used across various AI applications. In natural language processing (NLP), libraries like NLTK and spaCy offer robust tools for text analysis and language modeling. For computer vision, OpenCV and TensorFlow provide powerful capabilities for image and video processing. In data science, pandas and NumPy are indispensable for data manipulation and numerical analysis.

Let us consider a healthcare project where AI is used to predict patient outcomes based on historical data. Python's scikit-learn can be employed to create predictive models, while pandas and NumPy handle data preprocessing and analysis. The seamless integration of these tools allows for a smooth workflow from data ingestion to model deployment.

R

Strengths:

R is a language specifically designed for statistical computing and data analysis, making it a strong contender for AI projects that involve heavy data manipulation and statistical modeling. It boasts a comprehensive set of packages for data visualization, such as ggplot2 and lattice, which can help you create detailed and informative graphics to accompany your AI models.

R's strength lies in its ability to handle large datasets and perform complex statistical operations with ease. Its package ecosystem, including caret for machine learning and randomForest for ensemble learning, provides a solid foundation for developing AI applications.

Weaknesses:

Despite its strengths, R is not as versatile as Python when it comes to general-purpose programming. Its syntax can be less intuitive for those who are new to programming, and it lacks the extensive machine learning and deep learning libraries available in Python. Additionally, R's performance can be slower compared to other languages like C++ or Java, especially for computationally intensive tasks.

Use Cases and Applications:

R is particularly well-suited for AI projects in academia and research, where statistical analysis and data visualization are paramount. In fields like bioinformatics and social sciences, R's robust statistical capabilities allow researchers to build predictive models and conduct in-depth data analysis.

For example, in a social science study analyzing survey data to predict voting behavior, R can be used to preprocess the data, perform statistical tests, and build machine-learning models. The detailed visualizations created with ggplot2 can then help communicate the findings effectively.

JAVA

Strengths:

Java is a powerful, versatile language known for its performance and portability. It is widely used in enterprise environments and has a strong presence in the development of large-scale, high-performance applications. Java's robust framework for building distributed systems and its scalability make it a good choice for AI applications that need to handle substantial data processing workloads.

Java offers a variety of libraries and frameworks for AI development, such as Weka for machine learning and Deeplearning4j for deep learning. Its object-oriented nature promotes reusable and maintainable code, which is beneficial for complex AI projects.

Its extensive boilerplate code can slow down the development process, and the initial setup and configuration for AI libraries can be more cumbersome.

Use Cases and Applications:

Java is often used in developing AI applications that require integration with large-scale enterprise systems. In the financial industry, for instance, Java's performance and reliability make it suitable for building AI models that analyze market trends and predict stock prices.

Consider a financial application that uses machine learning to detect fraudulent transactions. Java's Weka library can be used to build and train the model, while its scalability ensures that the system can handle the large volumes of transactions processed daily.

C++

Strengths:

C++ is renowned for its performance and efficiency, making it a popular choice for developing AI applications that require high computational power and real-time processing. Its ability to interact closely with hardware allows for optimization at a low level, which is crucial for performance-critical applications.

C++ provides a high degree of control over system resources, which can be advantageous when implementing complex algorithms that need to run efficiently. Libraries like Dlib and TensorFlow (which has C++ bindings) enable developers to build high-performance AI models.

Weaknesses:

The complexity of C++ can be a significant barrier for beginners. Its syntax is more complicated than languages like Python or Java, and managing memory manually can introduce bugs and errors. Additionally, the development process can be slower due to the need for meticulous optimization and debugging.

Use Cases and Applications:

C++ is ideal for AI applications in fields like robotics, gaming, and real-time systems where performance is critical. In robotics, for example, AI models often need to process sensor data and make decisions in real time. The performance capabilities of C++ make it suitable for these demanding tasks.

Imagine a robotic system that navigates and interacts with its environment. Using C++, developers can optimize the algorithms for pathfinding and obstacle detection, ensuring the robot responds swiftly and accurately to changes in its surroundings.

JULIA

Strengths:

Julia is a relatively new language designed for high-performance numerical computing, making it a strong candidate for AI and machine learning tasks. It combines the ease of use of Python with the speed of C++, offering the best of both worlds. Julia's syntax is simple and expressive, which helps in writing clear and concise code.

One of Julia's standout features is its performance. It is designed to be as fast as C and Fortran, making it suitable for computationally intensive AI applications. Julia's ability to call Python, C, and Fortran libraries directly also enhances its versatility.

Weaknesses:

Despite its strengths, Julia is still growing in terms of community support and the availability of AI libraries. While it has a rapidly expanding ecosystem, it doesn't yet match the extensive library support available in Python. This can limit its use in certain AI applications.

Use Cases and Applications:

Julia is particularly well suited for AI projects that require heavy numerical computation, such as scientific research and simulations. In fields like physics and engineering, Julia's performance and ease of use allow researchers to develop and test AI models efficiently.

For example, in climate modeling, where large-scale simulations are used to predict weather patterns, Julia's performance capabilities can handle the complex calculations required. Researchers can develop AI models that analyze climate data and provide accurate forecasts, benefiting from Julia's speed and numerical accuracy.

Choosing the right programming language for your AI projects is a crucial decision that can impact your productivity, the complexity of the problems you can solve, and the ease with which you can implement your solutions. Each language has its strengths and weaknesses, and the best choice depends on your specific needs and the nature of your project.

SETTING UP YOUR CODING ENVIRONMENT

Setting up a coding environment might sound scary, but it is a straightforward process with the right guidance. Here is a systematic approach to get you started on the right foot.

Step 1: Installing Python

Python is the go-to language for AI development due to its simplicity and the extensive range of libraries available for AI and machine learning (ML). To start, you need to install Python on your computer.

1. Download Python:

Visit the official Python website at python.org.

Navigate to the Downloads section.

Choose the version compatible with your operating system (Windows, macOS, or Linux). For beginners, the latest stable release is recommended.

2. Run the Installer:

Open the downloaded installer file.

Ensure you check the box that says "Add Python to PATH" before clicking the install button. This step is crucial as it allows you to run Python from the command line.

Follow the prompts to complete the installation process.

3. Verify Installation:

Open a command prompt (Windows) or terminal (macOS/Linux).

Type `python --version` or `python3 --version` to check if Python was installed correctly. You should see the version number displayed.

Step 2: Installing Essential Libraries

Libraries are collections of pre-written code that can help you perform common tasks. For AI development, several libraries are essential:

1. pip:

pip is Python's package installer. It usually comes pre-installed with Python.

You can check if pip is installed by typing `pip --version` in your command prompt or terminal.

2. Numpy and Pandas:

Numpy is essential for numerical computations.

Pandas is great for data manipulation and analysis.

Install them by running: `pip install numpy pandas`

3. Matplotlib and Seaborn:

These are used for data visualization.

Install them by running: `pip install matplotlib seaborn`

4. Scikit-learn:

A library for machine learning algorithms.

Install it by running: `pip install scikit-learn`

5. TensorFlow and Keras:

TensorFlow is a powerful library for deep learning, and Keras provides a user-friendly API for TensorFlow.

Install them by running: `pip install tensorflow keras`

Step 3: Choosing and Using an IDE

An Integrated Development Environment (IDE) can make your coding experience more efficient and enjoyable. Here are three popular IDEs for Python, each with unique features:

1. PyCharm:

PyCharm is a powerful IDE specifically designed for Python.

It offers intelligent code completion, real-time error checking, and a robust debugger.

Download and install PyCharm from jetbrains.com/pycharm.

Once installed, you can create a new project, configure your Python interpreter, and start coding.

2. Jupyter Notebook:

Jupyter Notebook is excellent for data science and AI, allowing you to write and execute code in a web-based interface.

Install it using `pip install notebook`.

Launch it by running `jupyter notebook` in your terminal. This command will open a new tab in your web browser where you can create and manage notebooks.

3. Visual Studio Code (VS Code):

VS Code is a versatile and lightweight code editor with many extensions available for Python development.

Download and install VS Code from code.visualstudio.com.

Install the Python extension for VS Code from the Extensions marketplace.

Configure your Python environment in VS Code to start coding.

Step 4: Tips for Troubleshooting Common Issues

Even with detailed instructions, you might encounter some hiccups. Here are a few common issues and how to resolve them:

1. Python Not Recognized in Command Line:

Ensure Python is added to your system's PATH.

Revisit the installer and look for the "Add Python to PATH" option.

2. Permission Errors:

On some systems, you might need administrative privileges to install certain packages. Try running the command prompt or terminal as an administrator.

3. Library Installation Errors:

Sometimes, library installations can fail due to network issues or conflicting versions. You can try upgrading pip using `pip install --upgrade pip` and then reinstalling the library.

4. IDE Configuration Issues:

Make sure your IDE is pointing to the correct Python interpreter. In PyCharm, you can configure the interpreter in the project settings. In VS Code, this is done through the Python extension settings.

5. Jupyter Notebook Not Launching:

Ensure that all dependencies are correctly installed. Sometimes, issues can be resolved by reinstalling Jupyter Notebook: `pip uninstall notebook` followed by `pip install notebook`.

By setting up your coding environment properly, you lay a solid foundation for your AI journey. It's like sharpening your knives before cooking – it makes the whole process smoother and more enjoyable. Now that your environment is ready, you're all set to start coding and walk around the fascinating world of coding with AI.

INTRODUCTION TO BASIC CODING CONCEPTS

Understanding basic coding concepts is the first step in becoming a proficient programmer. This section will introduce you to fundamental concepts such as variables, data types, and basic syntax. By the end, you will have written your first program and gained a foundational understanding of how coding works.

VARIABLES

Variables are like containers that store data. Imagine you have a box where you can put anything you want, label it, and refer to it whenever you need the item inside. In coding, variables serve a similar purpose. They store values that you can use and manipulate throughout your program.

For example, in Python, you can create a variable simply by assigning a value to a name:

```python
name = "Alice"
age = 30
height = 5.5
```

In this example, `name` is a variable that stores the string `"Alice"`, `age` stores the integer `30`, and `height` stores the float `5.5`.

DATA TYPES

Data types define the kind of data a variable can hold. You have to understand this because they determine what operations you can perform on the data. Let us look at some common data types in Python:

Integers: Whole numbers without a decimal point. For example, `5`, `-3`, `42`.

```python
number = 10
```

Floats: Numbers with a decimal point. For example, `3.14`, `-0.001`, `2.0`.

```python
pi = 3.14
```

Strings: Sequences of characters enclosed in quotes. For example, `"Hello, World!"`, `'Python'`.

```python
greeting = "Hello, World!"
```

Lists: Ordered collections of items, which can be of different data types, enclosed in square brackets. For example, `[1, 2, 3]`, `["apple", "banana", "cherry"]`.

```python
fruits = ["apple", "banana", "cherry"]
```

BASIC SYNTAX

Syntax refers to the set of rules that defines the combinations of symbols that are considered to be correctly structured programs in a language. Python has a straightforward and readable syntax. These are some basic rules:

Case Sensitivity: Python is case-sensitive. For example, `Variable` and `variable` are considered different identifiers.

```python
Variable = 5
variable = 10
```

Indentation: Python uses indentation to define the scope of loops, functions, and other constructs. Consistent indentation is very important.

```python
if True:
    print("This is indented")
```

Comments: Comments are non-executable parts of the code used to explain what the code does. In Python, comments start with `#`.

```python
# This is a comment
```

WRITING YOUR FIRST PROGRAM

Now, let's write your first Python program: the classic "Hello, World!" This simple program will print the phrase "Hello, World!" to the screen, introducing you to the basic structure of a Python script.

1. Open Your Code Editor: Open your preferred code editor (VS Code or PyCharm) and create a new file named `hello_world.py`.

2. Write the Code: Type the following code into the file:

```python
# This program prints Hello, World!
print("Hello, World!")
```

3. Run the Program: Save the file and run it. In VS Code, you can run the program by right-clicking the file and selecting "Run Python File in Terminal". In PyCharm, you can click the green play button.

Explanation of the Code

Comments: The first line is a comment. It's good practice to include comments to describe what your code does.

Print Function: The second line uses the `print` function to display text on the screen.

The `print` function is a built-in function that outputs the specified message to the screen. The message to be printed is enclosed in parentheses and double quotes.

Common Errors and Troubleshooting

While writing your first program, you might encounter some common errors:

SyntaxError: EOL while scanning string literal: This error occurs if you forget to close the quotes around your string.

```python
print("Hello, World!)
```

Ensure both opening and closing quotes are present.

NameError: name 'print' is not defined: This happens if you misspell the `print` function.

```python
prnt("Hello, World!")
```

Check for typos and correct them.

IndentationError: unexpected indent: Python expects consistent indentation. This error will occur if your indentation is inconsistent.

```python
if True:
print("Hello, World!")
```

Ensure that the indented lines are properly aligned.

VARIABLES AND DATA TYPES IN ACTION

Now that you've written your first program, let's expand it to use variables and different data types.

1. Modify Your Code: Open `hello_world.py` and modify it as follows:

```python
# This program demonstrates variables and data types
name = "Alice"
age = 30
height = 5.5
fruits = ["apple", "banana", "cherry"]

print("Hello, " + name + "!")
print("You are " + str(age) + " years old.")
print("Your height is " + str(height) + " feet.")
```

```
print("Your favorite fruits are " + ", ".join(fruits) + ".")
```

2. Run the Program: Save and run the program as before.

Explanation of the Code

Variables: We create variables `name`, `age`, `height`, and `fruits` to store different types of data.

String Concatenation: We use the `+` operator to concatenate strings.

Type Conversion: The `str` function converts non-string data types to strings so they can be concatenated with other strings.

Joining Lists: The `join` method combines the elements of a list into a single string, with each element separated by a specified delimiter.

```python
print("Your favorite fruits are " + ", ".join(fruits) + ".")
```

Common Errors and Troubleshooting

Expanding your program can introduce new types of errors:

TypeError: can only concatenate str (not "int") to str: This occurs if you try to concatenate a string with a non-string type without converting it.

```python
print("You are " + age + " years old.")
```

Fix it by converting `age` to a string using `str(age)`.

AttributeError: 'int' object has no attribute 'join': This happens if you mistakenly call the `join` method on a non-list object.

```python
print("Your favorite fruits are " + ", ".join(age) + ".")
```

Ensure that you're calling `join` on a list.

USING AI TO HELP WITH CODING

Using AI tools like ChatGPT can make learning to code even easier and more interactive. You can use prompts to get explanations, code snippets, and solutions to problems you encounter. Let me show you how you can use ChatGPT to help with your coding tasks:

1. Understanding Concepts: If you're unsure about a concept, you can ask ChatGPT for an explanation.

Prompt: "Explain what a variable is in Python with an example."

Response from ChatGPT:

```
A variable in Python is used to store a value. It acts as a placeholder for data that can be changed throughout the program. For example:
```python
age = 25
name = "John"
height = 5.9
```
```

2. Writing Code Snippets: You can ask ChatGPT to write code for a specific task.

Prompt: "Write a Python program to print 'Hello, World!'"

Response from ChatGPT:

```python
# This program prints Hello, World!
print("Hello, World!")
```

3. Debugging Code: If you encounter an error, you can describe the error to ChatGPT and ask for help in fixing it.

Prompt: "I get a SyntaxError when trying to print 'Hello, World!'. Can you help me fix it?"

Response from ChatGPT:

> ```
> A SyntaxError typically occurs due to a typo or missing character in your code. Ensure that your print statement is correctly formatted with matching quotes. Here's the correct code:
> 
> ```python
> print("Hello, World!")
> ```

By using AI tools like ChatGPT, you can get instant help and guidance, making your learning process smoother and more efficient. Whether you need explanations, code examples, or debugging assistance.

Now that you understand these basic concepts and troubleshooting common errors, you build a solid foundation for more advanced programming tasks. As you continue to practice and explore, these foundational skills will serve you well, making your coding process more rewarding and enjoyable.

CHAPTER 3

PYTHON BASICS WITH AI ASSISTANCE

BASIC DATA STRUCTURES IN PYTHON

Python is a versatile and beginner-friendly programming language that has gained popularity due to its readability and simplicity. This chapter will introduce you to basic data structures in Python, such as lists, dictionaries, and tuples, and explain control structures like loops and conditionals. Additionally, we will look at how AI tools can assist in learning these concepts, providing a robust foundation for your programming journey.

LISTS

A list is an ordered collection of items, which can be of different data types. Lists are mutable, meaning their content can be changed after creation. They are useful for storing sequences of items.

Creating Lists: You can create a list by placing items inside square brackets, separated by commas.

```python
fruits = ["apple", "banana", "cherry"]
numbers = [1, 2, 3, 4, 5]
mixed = [1, "apple", 3.5, True]
```

Accessing List Elements: You can access elements by their index, starting from 0.

```python
print(fruits[0])  # Output: apple
print(numbers[2])  # Output: 3
```

Modifying Lists: Lists can be modified by assigning new values to specific indices.

```python
fruits[1] = "blueberry"
print(fruits)  # Output: ['apple', 'blueberry', 'cherry']
```

Iterating Over Lists: You can use loops to iterate over list elements.

```python
for fruit in fruits:
    print(fruit)
```

DICTIONARIES

A dictionary is an unordered collection of key-value pairs. Each key is unique, and values can be of any data type. Dictionaries are useful for storing related data.

Creating Dictionaries: You can create a dictionary by placing key-value pairs inside curly braces, separated by commas.

```python
student = {"name": "Alice", "age": 25, "grade": "A"}
```

Accessing Dictionary Elements: You can access values by their keys.

```python
print(student["name"])  # Output: Alice
print(student["age"])   # Output: 25
```

Modifying Dictionaries: You can add or modify key-value pairs.

```python
student["age"] = 26
student["major"] = "Computer Science"
print(student) # Output: {'name': 'Alice', 'age': 26, 'grade': 'A', 'major': 'Computer Science'}
```

Iterating Over Dictionaries: You can use loops to iterate over keys, values, or key-value pairs.

```python
for key, value in student.items():
    print(f"{key}: {value}")
```

TUPLES

A tuple is an ordered collection of items similar to a list, but unlike lists, tuples are immutable. They are useful for storing a collection of items that should not change.

Creating Tuples: You can create a tuple by placing items inside parentheses, separated by commas.

```python
coordinates = (10.0, 20.0)
colors = ("red", "green", "blue")
```

Accessing Tuple Elements: You can access elements by their index, just like lists.

```python
print(coordinates[0])  # Output: 10.0
print(colors[1])  # Output: green
```

Immutable Nature of Tuples: You cannot modify elements of a tuple.

```python
# This will raise an error
# coordinates[0] = 15.0
```

CONTROL STRUCTURES IN PYTHON

Loops

Loops are used to execute a block of code repeatedly. Python supports two types of loops: `for` and `while`.

For Loop: Iterates over a sequence (like a list, tuple, or string).

```python
for number in numbers:
    print(number)
```

Example: Print each fruit in the `fruits` list.

```python
for fruit in fruits:
    print(fruit)
```

While Loop: Repeats as long as a condition is true.

```python
count = 0
while count < 5:
    print(count)
    count += 1
```

Example: Count from 0 to 4.

```python
count = 0
while count < 5:
    print(count)
    count += 1
```

Conditionals

Conditionals are used to execute a block of code based on certain conditions. Python supports `if`, `elif`, and `else` statements.

If Statement: Executes a block of code if a condition is true.

```python
if age > 18:
    print("You are an adult.")
```

Elif Statement: Checks another condition if the previous conditions are false.

```python
if age < 13:
    print("You are a child.")
elif age < 18:
    print("You are a teenager.")
```

Else Statement: Executes a block of code if all previous conditions are false.

```python
if age < 13:
    print("You are a child.")
elif age < 18:
    print("You are a teenager.")
else:
    print("You are an adult.")
```

Example: Determine the category of a person based on age.

```python
age = 20
if age < 13:
    print("You are a child.")
elif age < 18:
    print("You are a teenager.")
else:
    print("You are an adult.")
```

CHAT GPT PROMPT SAMPLE

Understanding Lists

Prompt: "Explain what a list is in Python with examples."

Response from AI:

> ```
> A list in Python is an ordered collection of items that can be of different data types. For example:
> 
> ```python
> fruits = ["apple", "banana", "cherry"]
> numbers = [1, 2, 3, 4, 5]
> ```
> ```

Prompt: "How do I add an item to a list in Python?"

Response from AI:

> ```
> You can add an item to a list using the `append` method. For example:
> 
> ```python
> fruits.append("orange")
> print(fruits)  # Output: ['apple', 'banana', 'cherry', 'orange']
> ```
> ```

Understanding Dictionaries

Prompt: "What is a dictionary in Python and how do I use it?"

Response from AI:

```
A dictionary in Python is an unordered collection of key-value pairs. Each key is unique. For example:

```python
student = {"name": "Alice", "age": 25, "grade": "A"}
```
```

Prompt: "How can I add a new key-value pair to a dictionary?"

Response from AI:

```
You can add a new key-value pair by simply assigning a value to a new key. For example:

```python
student["major"] = "Computer Science"
print(student)  # Output: {'name': 'Alice', 'age': 25, 'grade': 'A', 'major': 'Computer Science'}
```
```

Understanding Tuples

Prompt: "Explain tuples in Python with examples."

Response from AI:

```
A tuple in Python is an ordered collection of items that is immutable. For example:

```python
coordinates = (10.0, 20.0)
colors = ("red", "green", "blue")
```
```

Understanding Loops

Prompt: "How do I use a for loop in Python?"

Response from AI:

```
A for loop in Python is used to iterate over a sequence. For example, to print each number in a list:

```python
numbers = [1, 2, 3, 4, 5]
for number in numbers:
    print(number)
```
```

Understanding Conditionals

Prompt: "Explain if-else statements in Python."

Response from AI:

```
If-else statements are used to execute code based on conditions. For example:

```python
age = 20
if age < 13:
    print("You are a child.")
elif age < 18:
    print("You are a teenager.")
else:
    print("You are an adult.")
```
```

PRACTICAL PROBLEMS FOR PRACTICE

To solidify your understanding of Python basics, try solving these practical problems on your own:

Problem: List Manipulation

- Create a list of your favorite movies.
- Add a new movie to the list.

- Remove the first movie from the list.
- Print the updated list.

Problem: Dictionary Operations

- Create a dictionary to store information about a book (title, author, year).
- Add a new key-value pair for the genre of the book.
- Update the year of the book.
- Print the updated dictionary.

Problem: Tuple Operations

- Create a tuple with the names of three cities.
- Print the name of the second city in the tuple.
- Try to change the name of the third city (expect an error).

Problem: Looping Through Lists

- Create a list of numbers from 1 to 10.
- Use a for loop to print each number in the list.
- Use a while loop to print each number in the list.

Problem: Conditional Statements

- Create a variable to store your age.
- Use an if-elif-else statement to print whether you are a child, teenager, or adult.

By working through these problems, you'll gain hands-on experience with Python's basic data structures and control structures. Keep practicing and experimenting with code, and don't hesitate to use AI as a valuable resource for learning and problem-solving. Happy coding!

CHAPTER 4

DEBUGGING CODE WITH CHATGPT

WHAT IS DEBUGGING?

Debugging is a fundamental part of the coding process, which is very essential for any aspiring programmer to master. Think of it as being a detective, but instead of solving crimes, you're hunting down and fixing errors in your code. Debugging is all about identifying and resolving issues to ensure your program runs smoothly and as intended.

At its core, debugging involves finding and fixing bugs in your code. Bugs are errors or unexpected behaviors that can cause a program to crash, produce incorrect results, or perform inefficiently. These issues can arise from various sources, such as typographical errors, logical flaws, or incorrect assumptions about how the code should function. The debugging process typically consists of identifying the bug, isolating its source, correcting the error, and testing the fix to ensure the problem is resolved without introducing new issues.

Debugging is important for several reasons. Firstly, it ensures the reliability and correctness of your code. Even the smallest bug can lead to significant problems, so debugging helps you eliminate these errors, making your code more robust. Additionally, debugging enhances your analytical and problem-solving skills, teaching you to think critically and systematically—abilities that are valuable beyond programming. Through debugging, you gain a deeper understanding of your code, which helps you write better and more efficient programs in the future. Regular debugging also makes your development process more efficient by catching issues early, reducing the time and effort required to fix them later.

The process of debugging can seem overwhelming initially, but following a structured approach can simplify it. Begin by reproducing the bug consistently, which helps you understand the conditions under which it occurs. Pay close attention to error messages or logs, as they often provide valuable clues about the problem's location and cause. Reviewing recent changes in your code can be particularly helpful if the bug is new, as issues often arise from modifications. Isolate the problem by narrowing down the section of code where the bug occurs, which you can do by systematically disabling parts of the code or using debugging tools to step through it line by line.

Understanding the problematic code section is also crucial. Sometimes, explaining the code to someone else or even to yourself out loud can help clarify the problem. Once you've pinpointed the source of the bug, make the necessary corrections methodically. After fixing the bug, test your code thoroughly to ensure the issue is resolved and no new problems have arisen. Finally, document the bug and the fix. This record will be invaluable for future reference and can aid other team members who might encounter similar issues.

COMMON CODING ERRORS AND HOW TO RESOLVE THEM

Learning to code is an exciting journey filled with creativity and problem-solving. However, along the way, you'll inevitably encounter errors that can be frustrating but are also fantastic learning opportunities. Let's examine some of the most common coding errors beginners face, including syntax errors, runtime errors, and logical errors. We'll investigate into specific pitfalls in Python and provide detailed step-by-step resolutions for each type of error. Consider this your friendly guide to debugging and improving your coding skills.

Syntax Errors

Syntax errors are like grammatical mistakes in a natural language. They occur when the code does not follow the rules of the programming language, making it impossible for the interpreter or compiler to understand. These errors are usually straightforward to identify and fix because they typically come with clear error messages.

Example:

```python
print("Hello, world!"
```

Here, there's a missing closing parenthesis.

Step-by-Step Resolution:

1. Read the Error Message: The Python interpreter will indicate a syntax error and point to the location of the issue.

2. Locate the Error: Check the line number mentioned in the error message.

3. Correct the Syntax: Add the missing closing parenthesis.

```python
print("Hello, world!")
```

Now, the code will run correctly, displaying "Hello, world!" on the screen.

Runtime Errors

Runtime errors occur when the program is running. They happen due to illegal operations like dividing by zero, accessing an out-of-bounds index, or working with undefined variables. These errors can be trickier to debug because they depend on the program's state and input at runtime.

Example:

```python
number = int(input("Enter a number: "))
print(10 / number)
```

If the user enters `0`, this will cause a `ZeroDivisionError`.

Step-by-Step Resolution:

1. Reproduce the Error: Run the program with various inputs to confirm the conditions under which the error occurs.

2. Read the Error Message: Python will raise a `ZeroDivisionError` and point to the offending line.

3. Add Error Handling: Implement a check to prevent illegal operations.

```python
number = int(input("Enter a number: "))
if number == 0:
    print("Cannot divide by zero.")
else:
    print(10 / number)
```

```
```

Now, if the user enters `0`, the program will print a helpful message instead of crashing.

Logical Errors

Logical errors are the most insidious because the code runs without crashing but produces incorrect results. These errors arise from flaws in the program's logic and can be difficult to spot because there are no error messages to guide you.

Example:

```python
def is_even(number):
    return number % 2 == 1
print(is_even(4))  # Expected: False, but returns True
```

The function incorrectly determines whether a number is even.

Step-by-Step Resolution:

1. Test the Function: Use various inputs to understand how the function behaves.

2. Identify the Logical Flaw: Realize that the condition `number % 2 == 1` checks for odd numbers, not even ones.

3. Correct the Logic: Modify the function to check for even numbers.

```python
def is_even(number):
    return number % 2 == 0


print(is_even(4))  # Expected: False, returns False
```

With the corrected logic, the function now returns the expected results.

COMMON PITFALLS IN PYTHON

Python is a powerful and beginner-friendly language, but it has its quirks. Let's explore some common pitfalls and how to avoid them.

Indentation Errors:

Python uses indentation to define code blocks. Inconsistent indentation can lead to `IndentationError`.

Example:

```python
def greet():
print("Hello, world!")  # Incorrect indentation
```

Step-by-Step Resolution:

1. Read the Error Message: Python will indicate an `IndentationError` and show where the problem is.

2. Check Indentation Levels: Ensure all code blocks have consistent indentation.

3. Correct the Indentation: Properly indent the code block.

```python
def greet():
    print("Hello, world!")
```

Mutable Default Arguments:

Using mutable default arguments in functions can lead to unexpected behavior.

Example:

```python
def add_item(item, item_list=[]):
    item_list.append(item)
    return item_list


print(add_item(1))  # Expected: [1], prints [1]
print(add_item(2))  # Expected: [2], prints [1, 2]
```

Step-by-Step Resolution:

1. Understand the Behavior: Realize that the default list is shared across function calls.

2. Use Immutable Defaults: Use `None` as the default and create a new list inside the function.

```python
def add_item(item, item_list=None):
    if item_list is None:
        item_list = []
    item_list.append(item)
    return item_list
```

```
print(add_item(1))  # Expected: [1], prints [1]
print(add_item(2))  # Expected: [2], prints [2]
```

Off-by-One Errors:

These occur frequently in loops and can cause incorrect indexing or range issues.

Example:

```python
numbers = [1, 2, 3, 4, 5]
for i in range(len(numbers)):
    print(numbers[i+1])  # This will cause an IndexError on the last iteration
```

Step-by-Step Resolution:

1. Identify the Error: Recognize that `i+1` will go out of bounds on the last iteration.

2. Adjust the Loop: Modify the loop to prevent out-of-bounds access.

```python
numbers = [1, 2, 3, 4, 5]
for i in range(len(numbers) - 1):
    print(numbers[i+1])  # This now works correctly
```

Type Errors:

Mixing data types in operations can lead to `TypeError`.

Example:

```python
number = input("Enter a number: ")
print(number + 10)  # This will cause a TypeError
```

Step-by-Step Resolution:

1. Understand Data Types: Realize that `input()` returns a string.

2. Convert Data Types: Convert the input to an integer before performing arithmetic operations.

```python
number = int(input("Enter a number: "))
print(number + 10)  # This now works correctly
```

Name Errors:

Using variables that haven't been defined leads to `NameError`.

Example:

```python
print(message)   # NameError because 'message' is not defined
```

Step-by-Step Resolution:

1. Identify the Error: Recognize that `message` has not been defined.

2. Define the Variable: Ensure the variable is defined before use.

```python
message = "Hello, world!"
print(message)
```

Attribute Errors:

Trying to access an attribute or method that doesn't exist results in `AttributeError`.

Example:

```python
class Dog:
    def __init__(self, name):
        self.name = name

dog = Dog("Buddy")
print(dog.age)  # AttributeError because 'age' is not defined
```

Step-by-Step Resolution:

1. Identify the Error: Realize that the `Dog` class does not have an `age` attribute.

2. Add the Attribute: Define the missing attribute in the class.

```python
class Dog:
    def __init__(self, name, age):
        self.name = name
        self.age = age

dog = Dog("Buddy", 5)
```

```
print(dog.age)  # This now works correctly
```

Index Errors:

Accessing a list with an invalid index results in `IndexError`.

Example:

```python
numbers = [1, 2, 3]
print(numbers[3])   # IndexError because index 3 is out of range
```

Step-by-Step Resolution:

1. Identify the Error: Recognize that the index is out of range.

2. Validate the Index: Check the index before accessing the list.

```python
numbers = [1, 2, 3]
if len(numbers) > 3:
    print(numbers[3])
else:
    print("Index out of range")
```

USING CHATGPT TO DEBUG CODE

Debugging is a fundamental skill for any programmer. While it can be a big task for beginners, tools like ChatGPT can significantly ease the process. This advanced AI model can help identify and fix errors in your code, explain complex concepts, and suggest improvements. Think of it as a friendly mentor who is always available to assist you.

ChatGPT, developed by OpenAI, is an advanced language model designed to understand and generate human-like text. When it comes to debugging, it can:

1. Identify Errors: Quickly spot syntax or logical errors in your code.

2. Provide Explanations: Explain why an error is occurring and suggest how to fix it.

3. Suggest Improvements: Offer advice on optimizing or refactoring your code.

4. Clarify Concepts: Help you understand programming concepts that might be causing issues.

To get the most out of ChatGPT, it's essential to interact with it effectively:

Be Specific: Clearly state the problem you are facing and provide context. General questions like "Why isn't my code working?" are less effective than specific ones that mention the error message or describe the unexpected behavior.

Include Code Snippets: When asking for help with code, always include the relevant portions of your code. This helps ChatGPT understand the context and provide precise solutions.

Ask Follow-up Questions: If the initial response isn't clear or doesn't fully solve your problem, don't hesitate to ask follow-up questions. Clarify any doubts you have about the explanation or solution provided.

Test the Solution: After receiving a response, implement the suggested changes in your code and test to see if the issue is resolved. Learning by doing is crucial for solidifying your understanding.

Framing Effective Questions

The quality of the responses you receive from ChatGPT largely depends on how well you frame your questions. Let me give you some tips for framing questions effectively:

1. Describe the Problem Clearly: Start by describing the issue you are facing in detail. Include the specific error message you are getting or describe the unexpected behavior of your program.

2. Provide Relevant Code: Include the part of your code that is causing the problem. Ensure the code snippet is complete enough for ChatGPT to understand the context but concise enough to focus on the issue.

3. State Your Intentions: Explain what you expect your code to do. This helps ChatGPT understand where your code is deviating from its intended behavior and provide more targeted advice.

4. Be Open to Suggestions: Sometimes, the solution might involve rethinking your approach or learning a new concept. Be open to exploring these suggestions, as they can provide valuable learning opportunities.

Interpreting Responses from ChatGPT

Once you receive a response from ChatGPT, it's essential to interpret and act on it effectively:

Read Carefully: Take your time to read and understand the explanation and the suggested solution. ChatGPT often provides detailed reasoning along with code snippets.

Implement and Test: Apply the suggested changes to your code and test to see if the issue is resolved. Debugging is often an iterative process, so be prepared to make adjustments.

Learn from the Interaction: Each interaction with ChatGPT is an opportunity to learn. Take note of the explanations and solutions to enhance your understanding. This will help you avoid similar mistakes in the future.

Ask for Clarification: If the response isn't entirely clear, don't hesitate to ask for further clarification. A good mentor is always willing to explain things in different ways until you understand.

Leveraging ChatGPT for Learning

Beyond fixing immediate errors, ChatGPT can be a valuable tool for continuous learning:

Ask for Explanations: Don't just seek solutions; ask for explanations to understand the underlying concepts. This deepens your knowledge and helps you become a more proficient programmer.

Explore Alternatives: Inquire about alternative approaches to solving a problem. This broadens your understanding and exposes you to different coding techniques.

Seek Best Practices: Use ChatGPT to learn about best practices and coding standards. This improves the quality and readability of your code, making you a more effective programmer.

Benefits of Using ChatGPT for Debugging

Immediate Assistance: ChatGPT provides instant feedback, helping you quickly identify and fix errors. This reduces downtime and keeps you productive.

Comprehensive Explanations: ChatGPT offers detailed explanations, helping you understand not just what to do, but why. This enhances your problem-solving skills and coding knowledge.

Support for Multiple Languages: Whether you're working with Python, JavaScript, or another language, ChatGPT can assist you. Its versatility makes it a valuable resource for learning different programming languages and paradigms.

Learning New Concepts: By interacting with ChatGPT, you can learn new programming concepts and techniques. This ongoing learning process is essential for growth as a programmer.

Confidence Building: Successfully debugging code with the help of ChatGPT builds your confidence. As you become more adept at identifying and resolving issues, you'll become more self-reliant and proficient.

DEBUGGING TOOLS AND TECHNIQUES

As a beginner, learning effective debugging techniques and familiarizing yourself with various debugging tools can significantly enhance your problem-solving skills and boost your confidence as a programmer. In this section, we will look at several debugging tools and techniques, including integrated development environment (IDE) debuggers, print statements, logging, and version control systems like Git. We will provide detailed examples and scenarios to demonstrate when and how to use these tools effectively.

IDE Debuggers

Integrated Development Environments (IDEs) like PyCharm, Visual Studio Code, and Eclipse come with built-in debuggers that offer a wide range of functionalities. These debuggers allow you to pause the execution of your code, inspect variables, and step through your code line by line. This helps you understand the flow of your program and identify where things might be going wrong.

Example Scenario: Stepping Through Code

Imagine you have a function that sorts a list of numbers, but it's not producing the expected results. By using an IDE debugger, you can set breakpoints at key points in your code and step through each line to observe the values of variables and the flow of execution.

1. Set Breakpoints: Place breakpoints at the start of your function and at critical points where you suspect the issue might be.

2. Run the Debugger: Start your program in debug mode. The execution will pause at each breakpoint.

3. Inspect Variables: As you step through the code, inspect the values of variables to ensure they are what you expect.

4. Step Through Code: Use the step-over, step-into, and step-out features to navigate through your code. This helps you identify exactly where the logic breaks down.

Benefits:

Allows you to see the state of your program at any point in time.

Helps in understanding complex code flows and interactions.

Provides a visual representation of variable states and changes.

Print Statements

Print statements are a simple yet powerful debugging technique. By inserting print statements at various points in your code, you can output the values of variables and track the execution flow. This method is particularly useful for quickly checking the state of your program without setting up a more complex debugging environment.

Example Scenario: Tracking Variable Values

Suppose you have a loop that processes items in a list, but the results are incorrect. You can insert print statements to output the values of the variables inside the loop.

```python
numbers = [1, 2, 3, 4, 5]
squares = []
for num in numbers:
    print(f"Processing number: {num}")   # Debug print statement
    squares.append(num num)
print(f"Squares: {squares}") # Final output
```

Benefits:

Quick and easy to implement.

Requires no additional tools or setup.

Provides immediate feedback on variable states and program flow.

Logging

Logging is a more advanced and structured way of tracking events in your code compared to print statements. By using a logging library, you can control the level of detail in your output, filter messages, and write logs to files for later analysis. Logging is particularly useful for larger projects or when debugging issues in production environments.

Example Scenario: Detailed Event Tracking

Imagine you are developing a web application and need to track user actions and errors. Using Python's built-in logging module, you can create log entries at different levels (DEBUG, INFO, WARNING, ERROR, CRITICAL) to capture detailed information about the application's behavior.

```python
import logging

# Configure logging
logging.basicConfig(level=logging.DEBUG, filename='app.log', filemode='w',
            format='%(name)s - %(levelname)s - %(message)s')
```

```
def process_user_input(input_value):
    logging.info(f"Received input: {input_value}")
    if not input_value:
        logging.error("No input provided")
        return "Error: No input"
    result = f"Processed {input_value}"
    logging.debug(f"Processing result: {result}")
    return result

user_input = "Test"
output = process_user_input(user_input)
logging.info(f"Output: {output}")
```

Benefits:

Provides a systematic way to capture and analyze program behavior.

Allows for different levels of verbosity and filtering.

Can be directed to various outputs (console, files, remote servers).

Version Control Systems: Git

Version control systems like Git are essential tools for tracking changes in your codebase, collaborating with others, and managing different versions of your projects. Git enables you to revert to previous states of your code, compare changes, and branch out to experiment with new features or fixes without affecting the main codebase.

Example Scenario: Reverting Changes

Suppose you made several changes to your code, but now it's not working, and you're not sure which change caused the problem. With Git, you can review your commit history and revert to a previous state.

1. Commit History: Use `git log` to view the commit history and identify a stable state.

2. Revert Changes: Use `git checkout` or `git revert` to revert to the desired commit.

3. Branching: Create a new branch to experiment with fixes without affecting the main branch.

```bash
# View commit history
git log


# Revert to a previous commit
git checkout <commit_hash>


# Create a new branch for experimentation
git checkout -b debug-branch
```

Benefits:

Tracks all changes and allows you to revert to previous states.

Facilitates collaboration and code reviews.

Enables branching for isolated development and debugging.

Unit Testing

Unit testing involves writing tests for individual units of your code, typically functions or methods, to ensure they work as expected. By running these tests, you can quickly identify when and where your code breaks. Tools like pytest (Python) or JUnit (Java) can automate this process.

Example Scenario: Testing Function Outputs

Imagine you have a function that calculates the factorial of a number. By writing unit tests, you can verify that the function handles various inputs correctly.

```python
def factorial(n):
    if n == 0:
        return 1
    return n  factorial(n-1)

# Unit tests
def test_factorial():
    assert factorial(0) == 1
    assert factorial(5) == 120
    assert factorial(7) == 5040

# Run tests
test_factorial()
print("All tests passed.")
```

Benefits:

Ensures individual units of code work correctly.

Facilitates early detection of bugs.

Supports refactoring by providing a safety net of tests.

Code Reviews

Code reviews involve having other developers review your code before it's merged into the main codebase. This practice not only helps catch bugs but also improves code quality through collective insights and adherence to best practices.

Example Scenario: Collaborative Debugging

You've written a complex piece of code and want to ensure it's robust. By submitting your code for review, your peers can provide feedback, identify potential issues, and suggest improvements.

1. Submit Code: Push your changes to a feature branch and open a pull request.

2. Receive Feedback: Collaborators review the code, provide comments, and suggest changes.

3. Incorporate Feedback: Address the feedback and update your code accordingly.

Benefits:

Catches bugs and issues early.

Promotes knowledge sharing and adherence to best practices.

Enhances code quality and maintainability.

Automated Debugging Tools

Automated debugging tools like Pylint for Python or ESLint for JavaScript can analyze your code and flag potential errors, stylistic issues, and violations of coding standards. These tools integrate with IDEs and CI/CD pipelines to provide continuous feedback.

Example Scenario: Static Code Analysis

Suppose you want to ensure your Python code adheres to PEP 8 standards and is free of common errors. Using Pylint, you can automatically check your code for issues.

```bash
# Install Pylint
pip install pylint

# Run Pylint on your code
pylint your_script.py
```

Benefits:

Provides immediate feedback on code quality and potential errors.

Enforces coding standards and best practices.

Integrates with development workflows for continuous improvement.

By mastering these tools and techniques, you can approach debugging with confidence and improve the overall quality and reliability of your code.

CHAPTER 5

ADVANCED CODING TECHNIQUES WITH CHATGPT

WORKING WITH DATABASES AND APIS

In the world of software development, databases and APIs are essential components that help applications store, retrieve, and exchange data. Understanding how to work with databases and APIs is crucial for any aspiring developer. This section will cover the basics of databases, including SQL and NoSQL, how to connect to databases using code, and how to perform CRUD operations. Additionally, we'll explain what APIs are, how to interact with them, and provide examples of common API use cases. We will also demonstrate how ChatGPT can assist in writing and understanding database queries and API calls. Let's dive in!

Databases: The Basics

Databases are systems used to store, manage, and retrieve data efficiently. They are categorized into two main types: SQL (Structured Query Language) databases and NoSQL (Not Only SQL) databases.

SQL Databases

SQL databases are relational databases that store data in tables with rows and columns. Each table has a schema that defines the structure of the data. SQL is used to perform operations like querying, updating, and managing the data.

Popular SQL Databases: MySQL, PostgreSQL, SQLite, Microsoft SQL Server.

CRUD Operations: Create, Read, Update, Delete operations are fundamental to interacting with SQL databases.

NoSQL Databases

NoSQL databases are non-relational databases that store data in a variety of formats, such as key-value pairs, documents, graphs, or wide-column stores. They are designed for scalability and flexibility, often used for handling large volumes of unstructured data.

Popular NoSQL Databases: MongoDB, Cassandra, Redis, CouchDB.

Data Models: NoSQL databases use different data models such as document-oriented (MongoDB), key-value (Redis), and column-family (Cassandra).

Connecting to Databases Using Code

To interact with databases programmatically, you need to establish a connection using a database client or library specific to the programming language you are using. Let's look at examples in Python.

Connecting to an SQL Database

Using the `sqlite3` library in Python, you can connect to an SQLite database:

```python
import sqlite3

# Connect to the database (creates it if it doesn't exist)
conn = sqlite3.connect('example.db')

# Create a cursor object
cursor = conn.cursor()

# Create a table
cursor.execute('''CREATE TABLE IF NOT EXISTS users (id INTEGER PRIMARY KEY, name TEXT, age INTEGER)''')

# Commit the changes and close the connection
conn.commit()
conn.close()
```

Connecting to a NoSQL Database

Using the `pymongo` library in Python, you can connect to a MongoDB database:

```python
from pymongo import MongoClient

# Connect to the MongoDB server
client = MongoClient('localhost', 27017)

# Select the database
db = client['example_db']

# Select the collection (similar to a table in SQL)
collection = db['users']

# Insert a document into the collection
collection.insert_one({'name': 'Alice', 'age': 30})
```

Performing CRUD Operations

CRUD operations are fundamental to interacting with databases. Let's look at how to perform these operations in SQL and NoSQL databases.

SQL CRUD Operations

1. Create: Inserting data into a table.

```python
cursor.execute("INSERT INTO users (name, age) VALUES (?, ?)", ('Bob', 25))
```

2. Read: Querying data from a table.

```python
cursor.execute("SELECT FROM users")
rows = cursor.fetchall()
for row in rows:
    print(row)
```

3. Update: Modifying existing data.

```python
cursor.execute("UPDATE users SET age = ? WHERE name = ?", (26, 'Bob'))
```

4. Delete: Removing data from a table.

```python
cursor.execute("DELETE FROM users WHERE name = ?", ('Bob',))
```

NoSQL CRUD Operations

1. Create: Inserting a document into a collection.

```python
collection.insert_one({'name': 'Bob', 'age': 25})
```

2. Read: Querying documents from a collection.

```python
user = collection.find_one({'name': 'Bob'})
print(user)
```

3. Update: Modifying existing documents.

```python
collection.update_one({'name': 'Bob'}, {'$set': {'age': 26}})
```

4. Delete: Removing documents from a collection.

```python
collection.delete_one({'name': 'Bob'})
```

What are APIs?

APIs (Application Programming Interfaces) are sets of rules and protocols that allow different software applications to communicate with each other. APIs define the methods and data formats that applications can use to request and exchange information.

APIs can be broadly categorized into:

RESTful APIs: Use HTTP requests to perform CRUD operations. They are stateless and often use JSON or XML for data interchange.

GraphQL APIs: Allow clients to request only the data they need, providing more flexibility compared to RESTful APIs.

Interacting with APIs

To interact with APIs, you typically make HTTP requests using methods such as GET, POST, PUT, and DELETE. Here's how to interact with a RESTful API using Python's `requests` library.

GET Request

To retrieve data from an API:

```python
import requests

response = requests.get('https://api.example.com/users')
if response.status_code == 200:
    users = response.json()
    for user in users:
        print(user)
```

POST Request

To send data to an API:

```python
new_user = {'name': 'Charlie', 'age': 28}
response = requests.post('https://api.example.com/users', json=new_user)
if response.status_code == 201:
    print("User created successfully.")
```

PUT Request

To update data via an API:

```python
updated_user = {'age': 29}
response = requests.put('https://api.example.com/users/1', json=updated_user)
if response.status_code == 200:
    print("User updated successfully.")
```

DELETE Request

To delete data via an API:

```python
response = requests.delete('https://api.example.com/users/1')
if response.status_code == 204:
    print("User deleted successfully.")
```

Common API Use Cases

APIs are used in various scenarios to enable functionality and data exchange between applications:

Weather Data: Access current weather conditions and forecasts.

Payment Processing: Integrate with payment gateways like PayPal or Stripe.

Social Media Integration: Post updates or retrieve data from platforms like Twitter and Facebook.

Geolocation Services: Use services like Google Maps to get location data.

Practical Example: Building a Simple API Client

Let's build a simple API client that interacts with a fictional API to manage a list of tasks. This example will demonstrate how to perform CRUD operations using API calls.

Fetching Tasks (GET Request)

```python
import requests

response = requests.get('https://api.example.com/tasks')
if response.status_code == 200:
    tasks = response.json()
```

```
    for task in tasks:
        print(task)
else:
    print("Failed to fetch tasks.")
```

Creating a New Task (POST Request)

```python
new_task = {'title': 'Learn Python', 'completed': False}
response = requests.post('https://api.example.com/tasks', json=new_task)
if response.status_code == 201:
    print("Task created successfully.")
else:
    print("Failed to create task.")
```

Updating a Task (PUT Request)

```python
updated_task = {'completed': True}
```

```
response = requests.put('https://api.example.com/tasks/1',
json=updated_task)
if response.status_code == 200:
    print("Task updated successfully.")
else:
    print("Failed to update task.")
```

Deleting a Task (DELETE Request)

```python
Response
=requests.delete('https://api.example.com/tasks/1')
if response.status_code == 204:
    print("Task deleted successfully.")
else:
    print("Failed to delete task.")
```

WRITING ALGORITHMS AND DATA STRUCTURES

When diving into the world of computer science, two pillars you'll frequently encounter are algorithms and data structures. They are the building blocks for writing efficient and effective code.

Algorithms are step-by-step procedures or formulas for solving problems. Imagine you have a recipe for baking a cake—each step in the recipe is like a step in an algorithm. Some of the most common algorithms you'll encounter are sorting and searching algorithms.

Sorting Algorithms

Sorting algorithms organize data in a particular order, usually ascending or descending.

Bubble Sort

Bubble sort repeatedly steps through the list, compares adjacent elements, and swaps them if they are in the wrong order. This process is repeated until the list is sorted. For example, when sorting [4, 2, 7, 1], bubble sort will compare 4 and 2, swap them to [2, 4, 7, 1], then compare 4 and 7, and so on until the list becomes [1, 2, 4, 7].

Selection Sort

Selection sort divides the list into two parts: the sorted part at the beginning and the unsorted part. It repeatedly selects the smallest (or largest) element from the unsorted part and moves it to the end of the sorted part. For instance, when sorting [29, 10, 14, 37, 13], selection sort will find the smallest element (10), swap it with the first element to get [10, 29, 14, 37, 13], then find the next smallest (13), swap it with the second element, and continue this process until the list is sorted.

Merge Sort

Merge sort is a divide-and-conquer algorithm that splits the list into smaller sublists until each sublist contains a single element, then merges these sublists to produce a sorted list. When sorting [38, 27, 43, 3, 9, 82, 10], merge sort splits it into [38, 27, 43, 3] and [9, 82, 10], further splits these into smaller sublists, then merges them back together in sorted order.

Searching Algorithms

Searching algorithms find the position of a target value within a list.

Linear Search

Linear search scans each element in the list until the target value is found or the end of the list is reached. For example, to find 5 in [4, 2, 7, 1, 5], linear search starts from the beginning and compares each element with 5, finding it at position 4.

Binary Search

Binary search works on sorted lists by repeatedly dividing the search interval in half. If the target value is less than the middle element, the search continues in the lower half; otherwise, it continues in the upper half. For instance, to find 22 in [1, 5, 8, 12, 15, 22, 30], binary search compares 22 with the middle element (12), finds 22 is greater, searches the upper half [15, 22, 30], and then finds 22 at position 5.

Data Structures: Organizing Data for Efficiency

Data structures are ways to store and organize data so that it can be accessed and modified efficiently. Some fundamental data structures include arrays, linked lists, stacks, and queues.

Arrays

Arrays are a collection of elements, each identified by an index, stored in contiguous memory locations. They are ideal for situations where you need quick access to elements by index. For example, storing daily temperatures for a week in an array like [70, 72, 68, 65, 74, 77, 73] allows you to quickly access the temperature on the 4th day by referencing temperatures[3], which gives you 65.

Linked Lists

Linked lists are a collection of elements called nodes, where each node contains a data value and a reference (or link) to the next node in the sequence. They are useful for dynamic data structures where elements are frequently inserted or deleted. A linked list can be singly linked, where each node points to the next node, or doubly linked, where each node points to both the next and the previous node. For example, a linked list of tasks could look like Task1 -> Task2 -> Task3. To add a new task (Task4) after Task2, you adjust the pointers to Task2 -> Task4 -> Task3.

Stacks

Stacks are a collection of elements that follow the Last In, First Out (LIFO) principle. Elements are added (pushed) and removed (popped) from the same end, called the top of the stack. They are ideal for situations where you need to reverse the order of operations or manage function calls. A common example is the browsing history in a web browser, where pages visited are stored in a stack like [Home, About, Services]. When you visit the Contact page, you push(Contact) onto the stack. To go back to the previous page, you pop() the top of the stack, returning to Services.

Queues

Queues are a collection of elements that follow the First In, First Out (FIFO) principle. Elements are added (enqueued) at the back and removed (dequeued) from the front. They are perfect for scenarios where you need to manage tasks in order, like processing requests or scheduling. For example, a line of customers in a bank could be represented as a queue: [Alice, Bob, Charlie]. When a new customer (David) arrives, you enqueue(David) to get [Alice, Bob, Charlie, David]. To serve the next customer, you dequeue() Alice, leaving [Bob, Charlie, David].

Bringing It All Together

To truly appreciate the power of algorithms and data structures, let's consider a practical example: implementing a simple to-do list application. We can choose a linked list to store the tasks since tasks might need to be added or removed frequently. To manage our to-do list, we implement basic operations such as adding a task by appending a new node to the end of the linked list, removing a task by deleting a node, and viewing tasks by traversing the linked list and printing each task. Here's a sample implementation in Python:

```python
class Node:
    def __init__(self, task):
        self.task = task
        self.next = None


class ToDoList:
    def __init__(self):
        self.head = None

    def add_task(self, task):
        new_node = Node(task)
        if not self.head:
            self.head = new_node
        else:
            current = self.head
            while current.next:
                current = current.next
            current.next = new_node

    def remove_task(self, task):
```

```python
        current = self.head
        previous = None
        while current and current.task != task:
            previous = current
            current = current.next
        if previous is None:
            self.head = current.next
        elif current:
            previous.next = current.next

    def view_tasks(self):
        current = self.head
        while current:
            print(current.task)
            current = current.next

# Usage
todo = ToDoList()
todo.add_task("Buy groceries")
todo.add_task("Clean the house")
todo.add_task("Pay bills")
```

```
todo.view_tasks()

todo.remove_task("Clean the house")

todo.view_tasks()
```

In this example, we created a `Node` class to represent each task and a `ToDoList` class to manage the linked list of tasks. We implemented methods to add, remove, and view tasks, showcasing how linked lists can be practically used. Understanding algorithms and data structures is crucial for writing efficient code and solving complex problems. Sorting and searching algorithms like bubble sort, selection sort, and binary search provide the tools to organize and find data. Fundamental data structures like arrays, linked lists, stacks, and queues offer ways to manage data effectively.

WEB DEVELOPMENT WITH CHATGPT

Web development is an exciting field that combines creativity and technology to build interactive websites and applications. Whether you're crafting a simple blog or a complex web application, understanding the basics of web development is crucial.

At its core, web development involves creating websites and applications that run on the web. The process typically includes three primary technologies: HTML, CSS, and JavaScript.

HTML (HyperText Markup Language)

HTML is the backbone of any website. It provides the structure of a webpage by defining elements such as headings, paragraphs, images, links, and more. Think of HTML as the skeleton of your web content.

For example, an HTML file might look like this:

```html
```html
<!DOCTYPE html>
<html lang="en">
<head>
   <meta charset="UTF-8">
   <title>My First Webpage</title>
</head>
<body>
   <h1>Welcome to My Website</h1>
   <p>This is a paragraph of text on my webpage.</p>
   <a href="https://www.example.com">Visit Example</a>
</body>
```
```

```
</html>
```

In this snippet, `<h1>` defines a heading, `<p>` a paragraph, and `<a>` a hyperlink.

CSS (Cascading Style Sheets)

CSS is used to style and layout web pages. It allows you to add colors, fonts, spacing, and other visual elements to your HTML structure, making your webpage look attractive and professional.

Here's an example of CSS:

```css
body {
    font-family: Arial, sans-serif;
    background-color: #f0f0f0;
    margin: 0;
    padding: 20px;
}

h1 {
    color: #333;
}
```

```
p {
    color: #666;
}
```

This CSS snippet styles the body of the webpage with a specific font and background color. It also sets the color for headings and paragraphs.

JavaScript

JavaScript is a programming language that adds interactivity to your website. With JavaScript, you can create dynamic content that responds to user actions, such as clicking a button or filling out a form.

A simple JavaScript example:

```javascript
document.addEventListener('DOMContentLoaded', function() {

document.getElementById('myButton').addEventListener('click', function() {
    alert('Button clicked!');
  });
});
```

```
```

In this code, when the webpage is loaded, an event listener is added to a button with the ID `myButton`. When the button is clicked, an alert box pops up with the message "Button clicked!".

Front-End Development

Front-end development involves creating the parts of a website that users interact with directly. This includes the layout, design, and interactivity of the site. Front-end developers primarily use HTML, CSS, and JavaScript, along with frameworks and libraries that make development faster and more efficient.

React

React is a popular JavaScript library for building user interfaces. It allows developers to create reusable UI components and manage the state of their applications efficiently. React makes it easy to build complex interfaces with minimal code.

Some basic example of a React component:

```javascript
import React from 'react';


function HelloWorld() {
```

```
    return (
      <div>
        <h1>Hello, World!</h1>
      </div>
    );
}


export default HelloWorld;
```

In this example, we import React and define a functional component called `HelloWorld` that returns a simple greeting message.

How ChatGPT Can Help

ChatGPT can be an invaluable resource for learning React and other front-end technologies. For instance, if you're stuck on a particular concept or error, you can ask ChatGPT for clarification or solutions.

You: "How do I pass data between React components?"

ChatGPT: "To pass data between React components, you can use props. Props are read-only attributes that are passed from a parent component to a child component. Here's a simple example:"

```javascript
import React from 'react';

function ChildComponent(props) {
  return <h1>{props.message}</h1>;
}

function ParentComponent() {
  return <ChildComponent message="Hello from Parent!" />;
}

export default ParentComponent;
```

"In this example, the `ParentComponent` passes a `message` prop to the `ChildComponent`, which then displays it."

Back-End Development

Back-end development involves working on the server-side of a web application. It includes managing databases, server logic, and integration with front-end code. Back-end developers use languages like Python, Ruby, PHP, and JavaScript (Node.js) to build and maintain the server, database, and application logic.

Node.js

Node.js is a JavaScript runtime built on Chrome's V8 JavaScript engine. It allows developers to use JavaScript for server-side scripting, enabling the development of full-stack applications using a single programming language.

Here's a simple example of a Node.js server using the Express framework:

```javascript
const express = require('express');
const app = express();
const port = 3000;

app.get('/', (req, res) => {
   res.send('Hello, World!');
});
```

```
app.listen(port, () => {
  console.log(`Server is running on http://localhost:${port}`);
});
```

In this example, we create an Express server that responds with "Hello, World!" when the root URL is accessed.

How ChatGPT Can Help

ChatGPT can assist with learning Node.js and back-end development by providing explanations, code snippets, and debugging help. For example:

You: "How do I connect to a MongoDB database using Node.js?"

ChatGPT: "To connect to a MongoDB database using Node.js, you can use the `mongoose` library. First, install `mongoose` using npm:

```
npm install mongoose
```

Then, you can use the following code to connect to your database:"

```javascript
const mongoose = require('mongoose');

mongoose.connect('mongodb://localhost:27017/mydatabase', { useNewUrlParser: true, useUnifiedTopology: true })
  .then(() => console.log('Connected to MongoDB'))
  .catch(err => console.error('Could not connect to MongoDB', err));
```

"In this example, we connect to a local MongoDB instance named `mydatabase`. Make sure to replace the connection string with your own database details."

Building Web Applications with ChatGPT

Building a web application involves combining front-end and back-end technologies to create a seamless user experience. ChatGPT can guide you through the entire process, from setting up your development environment to deploying your application.

Setting Up Your Development Environment

A typical web development environment includes a code editor (like Visual Studio Code), a version control system (like Git), and a package manager (like npm for Node.js).

You: "How do I set up a new React project?"

ChatGPT: "To set up a new React project, you can use Create React App, a tool that sets up a modern web development environment with no configuration. Run the following command in your terminal:

```
npx create-react-app my-app
```

Then, navigate to your project directory and start the development server:

```
cd my-app
npm start
```

This will start the development server and open your new React application in the browser."

Integrating Front-End and Back-End

Once you have your front-end and back-end set up, you'll need to integrate them. This usually involves making HTTP requests from your front-end to your back-end to fetch or send data.

You: "How do I make an HTTP request from a React component to a Node.js server?"

ChatGPT: "You can use the `fetch` API or a library like `axios` to make HTTP requests from a React component. Here's an example using `axios`:

First, install `axios`:

```
npm install axios
```

Then, you can use it in your React component like this:"

```javascript
import React, { useState, useEffect } from 'react';
import axios from 'axios';

function App() {
  const [data, setData] = useState(null);

  useEffect(() => {
    axios.get('http://localhost:3000/api/data')
      .then(response => {
        setData(response.data);
```

```
    })
      .catch(error => {
        console.error('There was an error fetching the data!', error);
      });
  }, []);

  return (
    <div>
      {data ? <pre>{JSON.stringify(data, null, 2)}</pre> : <p>Loading...</p>}
    </div>
  );
}

export default App;
```

"In this example, the `App` component makes a GET request to the Node.js server and displays the fetched data."

Learning New Frameworks

Web development is an ever-evolving field, and staying up-to-date with the latest frameworks and technologies is essential. ChatGPT can be a valuable resource for learning new frameworks like React or Node.js.

You: "What are some good resources to learn React?"

ChatGPT: "Here are some excellent resources to learn React:

1. Official React Documentation: The official documentation is a comprehensive resource that covers everything from basic concepts to advanced techniques.

2. React Tutorial for Beginners: FreeCodeCamp offers an interactive React tutorial that covers the fundamentals.

3. React Course on Codecademy: Codecademy provides a structured course that includes hands-on projects and quizzes.

4. React Projects on GitHub: Exploring open-source React projects on GitHub can give you practical insights and inspiration."

BEST PRACTICES AND PITFALLS TO AVOID WHEN CODING WITH CHATGPT

Optimizing code efficiency is crucial to ensure that your programs run smoothly and effectively. When working with ChatGPT, it's important to be mindful of best practices and common pitfalls that can impact the performance of your code. One key practice is to avoid using unnecessary code. ChatGPT can generate extensive lines of code, but not all of it may be essential for your needs. Carefully review the generated code to ensure it includes only what is necessary. Additionally, using appropriate data structures is vital. While ChatGPT can suggest various structures like arrays, lists, and hash tables, selecting the right one for your specific task is important for optimal performance. For instance, if fast lookups are needed, a hash table might be more efficient than an array.

Minimizing function calls is another important practice, as they can be costly in terms of time and memory. Aim to reduce the number of function calls, especially those that involve large data structures as parameters. Employing lazy evaluation, which evaluates expressions only when their values are needed, can also help reduce processing time and improve efficiency. It's also advisable to avoid global variables, as they can lead to unexpected results and are generally considered bad practice. Instead, use local variables and pass values between functions as needed.

Hard-coding values can make future updates to your code difficult. Instead, use variables and constants for values that might change over time. Thoroughly testing your code is essential, even when using a tool like ChatGPT that can generate a large volume of code. Ensure your code handles a variety of test cases and edge cases correctly to confirm it works as expected.

When coding with ChatGPT, being aware of common mistakes and pitfalls is crucial. Over-reliance on ChatGPT can be problematic since it's not perfect and may generate incorrect or inefficient code. Always verify and test the generated code. Proper input formatting is necessary because ChatGPT relies on well-formatted input to produce accurate code. Understanding the underlying code concepts is also important, as it allows you to effectively use and debug the code ChatGPT generates. Inadequate testing and validation can lead to issues, so ensure your code is thoroughly tested for correctness and efficiency.

To maximize the benefits of ChatGPT, start by defining clear and specific goals for your project. This helps in determining the right input data and the expected output. Using a high-quality, diverse, and well-structured training data set is essential for generating high-quality output. Fine-tuning ChatGPT for your specific use case can further enhance its accuracy and efficiency. Make sure to use appropriate input and output formats for your particular needs, and regularly monitor the output for any errors or inconsistencies. While ChatGPT is powerful, it should be used in conjunction with other tools and techniques to improve the overall accuracy and efficiency of your code. Staying updated with the latest developments and updates from OpenAI ensures you are using the most efficient version of ChatGPT.

By following these best practices and being mindful of common pitfalls, you can optimize the efficiency of your code and make the most out of ChatGPT in your coding projects.

CONCLUSION

Coding is a skill that opens doors to creativity, problem-solving, and innovation. With AI continuously evolving, the possibilities for learning and growth are limitless. Whether you're pursuing a career in technology, exploring a passion project, or simply enjoying the thrill of coding, AI remains a valuable ally on your journey.

Your feedback is invaluable to us! If this book has helped you gain insights into coding with AI and enriched your learning experience, we would greatly appreciate your positive review and rating. Your support will encourage others to embark on their own coding adventures with AI, ensuring they too can benefit from the knowledge and resources shared in this book.

Thank you for choosing to learn with us. Keep coding, keep exploring, and remember—AI is here to help you every step of the way.

Happy coding!

www.ingramcontent.com/pod-product-compliance
Lightning Source LLC
Chambersburg PA
CBHW071930210526
45479CB00002B/620